LEONARDO DA VINCI

BOOK FOR CURIOUS KIDS

Discovering the Fascinating Life of the Polymath Behind the Mona Lisa

MARK LYLANI

MARK LYLANI

TABLE OF CONTENTS

INTRODUCTION

Ever wondered how one man could master both art and science, creating masterpieces and inventing futuristic machines centuries ahead of his time? Have you ever imagined a mind so curious that it delved into everything from painting the most famous portrait in the world to dissecting bodies to understand human anatomy? What if you could take a journey into the life of this genius, discovering his secrets and exploring his world?

Welcome to "Leonardo Da Vinci Book for Curious Kids," where we unravel the extraordinary life of one of history's most fascinating figures. Leonardo Da Vinci wasn't just a painter; he was a visionary, an inventor, a scientist, and a curious mind that never stopped exploring. Through these pages, you'll travel back to Renaissance Italy, meeting young Leonardo in the charming town of Vinci, following him to the bustling art studios of Florence, and witnessing his groundbreaking work in Milan.

Each chapter of this book takes you deeper into Da Vinci's world, from his early sketches and artistic training to his innovative designs and scientific studies. You'll learn about his famous works like "The Last Supper" and the "Mona Lisa," and you'll discover how his curiosity led him to explore anatomy, engineering, and the natural world.

Leonardo's story is not just about his successes but also about his challenges and unfinished projects, offering a glimpse into the relentless pursuit of knowledge that defined his life.

Are you ready to unlock the mysteries of Leonardo Da Vinci? Get ready to be inspired by a genius whose ideas and creations continue to amaze and influence us today. Dive into the adventure, and let your curiosity lead the way!

MARK LYLANI

Birth and Early Childhood

Welcome to the incredible world of Leonardo da Vinci! In this chapter, we will dive into his early years and learn about his birth, childhood, family background, and early influences. Get ready to explore the fascinating life of one of the greatest artists and thinkers in history!

Leonardo da Vinci, one of the greatest geniuses in history, was born on April 15, 1452, in the picturesque village of Vinci, Italy. He was the son of Ser Piero da Vinci and Caterina. From a young age, Leonardo exhibited an insatiable curiosity and an extraordinary talent for art and science.

Leonardo's early childhood was spent in Vinci, where he had a loving family but limited opportunities for education. As a child, he showed a keen interest in nature and loved exploring the beautiful countryside around his home.

At the age of five, Leonardo moved to his father's house in Florence. There, he was exposed to art and education, which sparked his curiosity and fueled his creative talents. Leonardo's father recognized his son's potential and decided to provide him with the best education possible.

Leonardo's education was broad, as he studied a wide range of subjects, including mathematics, literature, music, and art. His father also encouraged him to develop his artistic skills by enrolling him as an apprentice to the renowned artist Andrea del Verrocchio.

Under Verrocchio's guidance, Leonardo learned various techniques and honed his artistic abilities. He studied painting, drawing, sculpture, and even metalworking. Leonardo's determination and dedication to his craft were evident during his apprenticeship, and he quickly became one of Verrocchio's most talented students.

During his early years, Leonardo developed an insatiable curiosity about the world. He spent hours observing plants, animals, and the movement of water. He filled countless notebooks with detailed drawings and observations of his surroundings. Although

Leonardo's formal education was limited, his natural curiosity and passion for learning were boundless.

Leonardo's childhood experiences in Vinci and Florence played a crucial role in shaping his interests and abilities. The beauty of the Italian landscape, combined with exposure to art and education, ignited a lifelong passion for exploration and discovery. These early years laid the foundation for Leonardo's future as a brilliant artist, scientist, and inventor.

Apprenticeship with Verrocchio

Leonardo da Vinci was a young boy with an insatiable curiosity who loved to observe and explore the world around him. When he turned fifteen, he had the opportunity to become an apprentice to the renowned artist Andrea del Verrocchio.

Verrocchio was not only a painter but also a skilled sculptor, goldsmith, and engineer. He recognized Leonardo's potential and took him under his wing, teaching him the art of painting and sculpture. Leonardo was thrilled to learn from such a talented master.

Under Verrocchio's guidance, Leonardo acquired many techniques and skills. He studied the human body, animals, and nature, as Verrocchio believed that a great artist needed to thoroughly understand the world. Leonardo diligently absorbed this knowledge.

One of the important skills Leonardo learned during his apprenticeship was the art of preparing paints and creating different colors. Verrocchio taught him how to grind pigments and mix them with egg yolk to create durable paint for use on canvas. Leonardo was fascinated by the process and eagerly experimented with various mixtures to achieve perfect shades and tones.

Verrocchio also instructed Leonardo in the technique of chiaroscuro, which involves using light and shadow to create depth and dimension in a painting. Leonardo practiced this technique by observing how light interacted with different objects, as well as the formation of shadows. He learned to employ these effects to make his paintings appear realistic and lifelike.

During his time with Verrocchio, Leonardo also had the opportunity to contribute to some of his master's renowned artworks. Notably, he had the privilege of adding one of the angels to a famous painting called "The Baptism of Christ." Verrocchio was impressed with Leonardo's skills and recognized his talent, granting the young apprentice this honor.

Leonardo's dedication and commitment during his apprenticeship set him apart from the other students. Verrocchio acknowledged his talent and encouraged him to explore different artistic styles and techniques. He even allowed Leonardo to undertake personal projects, giving him the freedom to express his creativity.

Leonardo's apprenticeship under Verrocchio lasted for six years. During this time, he honed his artistic skills and developed his own unique style. He keenly observed the world around him and utilized his observations to create beautiful and realistic paintings.

At the conclusion of his apprenticeship, Leonardo was ready to venture out on his own and continue his artistic journey. Armed with valuable lessons from Verrocchio, he possessed the confidence to pursue his own artistic visions.

Early Artistic Works

Under Verrocchio's guidance, Leonardo developed his artistic skills and techniques. He worked on various projects, including sculptures and paintings. One of his earliest known works is a drawing called "The Arno Valley," which he created around 1473. This piece showcased his talent for capturing landscapes.

Leonardo's dedication to his craft and relentless pursuit of knowledge led him to study human anatomy. He realized that to create realistic figures, he needed to understand the human body from the inside out. Leonardo began studying human anatomy by observing and sketching the muscles, organs, and bones. Through these anatomical studies, he gained a deep understanding of how the body worked, which greatly influenced his artistic style.

Another notable early work by Leonardo is "The Annunciation," a painting he completed around 1475. It portrays the biblical scene where the angel Gabriel appears to the Virgin Mary to announce that she will give birth to Jesus. Leonardo's attention to detail and ability to convey emotions are evident in this masterpiece. He used light and shadow to create a sense of depth and realism, bringing the figures to life.

During his time in Verrocchio's workshop, Leonardo also collaborated with his master on several projects. One such collaboration was the painting "The Baptism of Christ."

Scholars believe that Leonardo contributed to this artwork, potentially by painting one of the background angels. Even at a young age, his talent was recognized and appreciated by his peers.

Leonardo's early artistic works laid the foundation for the innovative techniques and styles he later developed. His keen eye for detail, his fascination with capturing the essence of life in his art, and his commitment to pushing boundaries helped shape the Renaissance period. His curiosity and thirst for knowledge enabled him to explore new techniques, such as sfumato, which created soft, smoky transitions between colors. These techniques revolutionized art and inspired future generations of artists.

MARK LYLANI

Move to Milan

After completing his apprenticeship with Verrocchio, Leonardo decided to leave Florence and seek new opportunities in Milan. He was eager to expand his skills and work on larger and more prestigious projects. Milan was also a city bustling with intellectual and artistic activity during the Renaissance.

Leonardo arrived in Milan around 1482 and swiftly gained recognition as a talented painter. The Duke of Milan, Ludovico Sforza, noticed Leonardo's skills and hired him as his court artist. This was a significant advancement for Leonardo, as he was now able to work on important commissions for the Duke.

During his time in Milan, Leonardo not only focused on painting but also explored other fields like engineering, architecture, and military technology. His diverse interests and skills made him a valuable asset to the Duke. Leonardo's scientific and technical knowledge allowed him to design innovative machines and inventions, showcasing his multidisciplinary talents during the Renaissance.

One of Leonardo's most famous works during his time in Milan is "The Last Supper." The painting, which portrays Jesus' last meal with his disciples, was commissioned by the Duke for the refectory of the Santa Maria delle Grazie monastery. Leonardo took great care in creating this masterpiece, studying human expression and gestures to capture the emotional depth of each figure.

Leonardo faced many challenges while working on "The Last Supper." He experimented with different painting techniques, including using tempera on dry plaster, which unfortunately led to the painting deteriorating over time. Despite these challenges, "The Last Supper" became a significant artistic achievement and a testament to Leonardo's skill as a painter.

In addition to "The Last Supper," Leonardo worked on various other projects in Milan. He designed elaborate machinery and weapons for the Duke, including plans for a flying machine, a giant crossbow, and an armored vehicle. Although many of these designs were never built, they showcased

Leonardo's innovative thinking and his ability to merge art and science.

Unfortunately, Leonardo's time in Milan was not without its share of difficulties. The city faced political unrest, and the Duke's reign was threatened. This led to unstable working conditions for Leonardo, as he had to adapt to the changing circumstances constantly. Despite these challenges, he continued to produce remarkable artwork and inventions.

Leonardo's move to Milan marked a significant turning point in his career. It was during this time that he truly flourished as an artist, engineer, and thinker. His contributions to art and science in Milan left a lasting impact and set the stage for his future accomplishments.

The Last Supper

The Last Supper is one of Leonardo da Vinci's most famous and iconic works of art. Painted on the wall of the dining hall in the Santa Maria delle Grazie monastery in Milan, Italy, this mural depicts the final meal of Jesus and his apostles before his crucifixion. It is not just a beautiful piece of art but also a significant moment in art history.

Working on such a large mural presented its own set of challenges for Leonardo. The wall itself measured about 29 feet wide, and he had to plan out the composition and positioning of each character carefully. The task required immense skill and attention to detail.

One of the biggest challenges Leonardo faced was finding the right models for the apostles. He spent a considerable amount of time searching for faces that embodied the characters he wanted to portray. He wanted each apostle to have a distinct personality, and finding models who could accurately represent them was no easy task.

Additionally, Leonardo wanted to capture the emotions and interactions between the apostles at this pivotal moment. He wanted to depict the shock, disbelief, and sadness that Jesus' announcement of betrayal had caused. This required him to study and analyze human expressions and body language carefully. He would often observe people in the streets of Milan, observing how they interacted with each other and expressed different emotions.

Another challenge for Leonardo was the medium he chose to paint the Last Supper. Instead of traditional fresco, which would have allowed him to work slowly and make corrections, he chose to experiment with a new technique called tempera on dry plaster. This technique proved to be challenging because it required him to work quickly and precisely, as the paint would dry rapidly.

Despite these challenges, Leonardo's genius as an artist and his dedication to perfection shone through in the finished mural. The Last Supper is a masterpiece of perspective, composition, and emotional portrayal. The way he used lines and perspective draws viewers' eyes toward Jesus at the center of the painting, emphasizing his importance in this moment.

This mural had a profound impact on the world of art. It was one of the earliest instances of using a one-point perspective in such a large-scale composition, making it a groundbreaking piece in the history of visual representation. Leonardo's attention to detail and his ability to capture human emotion also set new standards for artists in portraying scenes of this nature.

However, as time passed, the painting deteriorated due to various factors, such as the poor choice of medium and the monastery's neglect. Attempts have been made to restore and preserve the mural, but it remains a challenge due to the original colors fading away and some areas being lost forever.

Although the Last Supper has suffered physically over the centuries, its impact on art history remains undeniable. Even today, artists and art enthusiasts visit the Santa Maria delle Grazie monastery to see this remarkable work up close. Leonardo da Vinci's Last Supper continues to inspire and captivate people around the world, reminding us of his immense talent and contribution to the world of art.

It is vital to preserve and protect this work of art, as it not only holds historical and artistic value but also provides insight into the mind and talent of one of the greatest artists who ever lived.

The challenges faced by Leonardo while creating the Last Supper demonstrate his dedication to perfection and his ability to innovate new techniques. This mural serves as a testament to Leonardo's artistic genius and his lasting impact on art history.

Scientific and Anatomical Studies

Leonardo da Vinci was not only an artist but also a scientist. He had a deep curiosity about the world around him and loved to study and observe things. One of his most famous areas of study was anatomy, the study of the human body. He believed that by understanding the human body, he could better depict it in his artwork.

Leonardo began his study of anatomy by dissecting cadavers. A cadaver is a deceased human body used for scientific research. Leonardo wanted to understand how the muscles, bones, and organs worked together. He carefully studied each part, made detailed drawings, and wrote extensive notes.

One of Leonardo's most famous anatomical drawings is the "Vitruvian Man." The Vitruvian Man is a drawing of a man standing with his arms and legs outstretched inside a circle and a square. Leonardo used this drawing to study the proportions of the human body. He believed that the human body was perfectly created by nature, and he wanted to understand its symmetry and balance.

Leonardo's anatomical studies went beyond just the human body. He also studied the anatomy of animals, such as horses and birds. He wanted to understand how these creatures were designed and how their bodies functioned. Leonardo made detailed drawings of the bones, muscles, and organs of animals, capturing their intricate structures.

Interestingly, Leonardo's anatomical studies were not just for his own knowledge. He also shared his findings with other artists and scientists of his time. Leonardo created detailed drawings and wrote extensive notes about his observations, which he hoped would be useful to others in their own studies.

Leonardo's anatomical studies were groundbreaking in the field of science. His careful observations and detailed drawings helped to advance the understanding of the human body. Even today, his anatomical drawings are highly regarded for their accuracy and attention to detail.

In addition to his anatomical studies, Leonardo was also interested in other scientific areas, such as botany, geology, and engineering. He made observations and drew sketches of plants, rocks, and machines.

Leonardo's scientific and anatomical studies influenced not only his own artwork but also future advancements in science and medicine.

The Vitruvian Man

Leonardo da Vinci was not only a talented artist but also a keen observer of the world around him. One of his most famous illustrations, "The Vitruvian Man," is a perfect example of his curiosity and dedication to studying the human body.

Leonardo was fascinated by human anatomy, believing that understanding the proportions of the human body was essential to creating accurate and realistic art. He studied the works of ancient Greek and Roman architects, such as Vitruvius, who believed that the human body represented the ideal proportions of nature.

"The Vitruvian Man" is a drawing that showcases Leonardo's understanding of these ideal proportions. In the illustration, a naked man stands with his arms and legs outstretched, fitting perfectly within both a square and a circle. The square represents the earthly, while the circle symbolizes the divine.

Leonardo was meticulous in his measurements, ensuring that every detail of "The Vitruvian Man" adhered to the principles of proportion. He used his own body as a reference, meticulously recording the length and width of various body parts. These measurements were inspired by the writings of ancient scholars.

Through his studies, Leonardo concluded that the human body was a microcosm of the larger world. He believed that its proportions could be applied to architecture and design. By understanding and applying these principles, Leonardo sought to create harmony between the human body and the structures humans constructed.

The drawing also serves as a tribute to the intersection of science and art. Leonardo was not only a talented painter but also a skilled mathematician. He believed that art and science were interconnected and could be used to enhance each other.

One of the reasons "The Vitruvian Man" has become one of Leonardo's most famous works is its universal appeal. It represents the ideal human form, emphasizing the beauty and harmony found in nature. It is a testament to Leonardo's skills and his profound interest in human anatomy and mathematical proportions.

Today, "The Vitruvian Man" continues to

inspire artists, architects, and scientists alike. Its depiction of the human body's proportions is still considered a fundamental principle in these fields. Leonardo's curiosity and dedication to understanding the world around him have left a lasting impact on how we perceive and create art and design.

Thus, "The Vitruvian Man" stands as a testament to Leonardo da Vinci's genius, showcasing his unparalleled skill and his eternal fascination with the intricacies of human anatomy and mathematical proportions.

Return to Florence

Leonardo da Vinci was always a wanderer, constantly seeking new opportunities to learn and create. After spending almost two decades in Milan, he decided to return to his hometown of Florence in 1500.

Florence was a bustling city filled with artistic and intellectual energy, and Leonardo was eager to immerse himself once again in its vibrant atmosphere.

Upon his return, Leonardo was welcomed with open arms by the city's prominent figures and art patrons. He was commissioned to create a painting for the high altar of the San Bernardo chapel in the Palazzo della Signoria. Unfortunately, due to the unstable political climate and conflicts between Florence and Pisa, Leonardo's plans were put on hold.

Despite the setback, Leonardo kept himself busy by working on other projects. He started conducting detailed studies of human anatomy at the Hospital of Santa Maria Nuova. Through extensive dissections, he aimed to further his understanding of the human body and its intricate mechanisms.

During this time, Leonardo also began drawing plans for a flying machine, inspired by his observations of birds' flight. He believed that humans, with the right contraption, could also conquer the skies. Although he never built a working flying machine, his sketches and ideas laid the foundation for future aviation pioneers.

Leonardo's fascination with water and its movement also continued in Florence. He studied the Arno River, its currents, and the forces that shaped its flow. His observations would later influence his groundbreaking work on hydrodynamics and the construction of canals.

As the political situation in Florence stabilized, Leonardo's long-awaited commission for the San Bernardo chapel was finally given the green light. The painting, known as the "Adoration of the Magi," was a masterpiece in progress. However, Leonardo left it unfinished when he was invited to work for the powerful ruler Cesare Borgia.

Despite leaving the painting unfinished, Leonardo's time in Florence was not in vain. He immersed himself in his artistic and scientific interests, honing his skills and expanding his knowledge. He painted portraits, designed elaborate festival costumes, and even collaborated with fellow artists on various projects.

Leonardo's return to Florence marked a significant turning point in his career. The experiences and interactions he had during this time greatly influenced his later works. Even though he would leave again soon, his impact on the city's art scene and his contributions to the Renaissance were indelible.

Florence had always held a special place in Leonardo's heart. It was where he had received his early education and artistic training. Returning to the city allowed him to reconnect with his roots and rediscover the inspiration that first sparked his passion for art and invention.

Leonardo's time in Florence was marked by

exploration, experimentation, and a constant quest for knowledge. It was a period of growth and discovery that laid the groundwork for his future achievements.

MARK LYLANI

The Battle of Anghiari

Leonardo da Vinci was not just an artist and inventor, but he also had a great interest in military engineering. In 1505, he was commissioned by the Republic of Florence to create a large mural depicting the Battle of Anghiari, which took place in 1440 between Florence and Milan.

The Battle of Anghiari was an important event during the Italian Wars, a series of conflicts between different city-states in Italy. It was fought near the Tuscan town of Anghiari between the forces of Florence, led by Niccolò Piccinino, and those of Milan, led by Count Francesco Piccinino.

Leonardo was excited about this commission because it allowed him to explore his passion for anatomy and motion. He wanted to capture the intensity and energy of the battle scene but also show the complexity and dynamics of the human body in action.

He started by carefully studying the anatomy of horses and soldiers, making detailed sketches of their movements and positions. He also studied human and animal bodies to understand their internal structures better. This knowledge enabled him to create more realistic and lifelike figures in his artwork.

Leonardo worked on the mural for several months, experimenting with different techniques and compositions. He used a new method of fresco painting, which involves applying pigments onto wet plaster. However, due to various technical difficulties and the experimental nature of his work, the mural was never completed.

Despite the unfinished mural, the Battle of Anghiari project had a profound impact on other artists of the time. Leonardo's sketches and studies became famous and were highly admired by his contemporaries, including Michelangelo, who later created his own version of the Battle of Cascina.

Unfortunately, Leonardo's original mural was lost over time. Attempts to uncover it in the Palazzo Vecchio in Florence have been made, but to this day, it remains hidden. However, copies and reproductions of the mural's composition and some of Leonardo's sketches still exist, giving us a glimpse into his artistic genius.

The Battle of Anghiari project demonstrated Leonardo's ability to combine his artistic skills with his scientific observations. His fascination with the human body and his understanding of anatomy allowed him to create more realistic and dynamic figures in his artwork.

Leonardo's dedication to the Battle of Anghiari reflects his passion for capturing the essence of movement and life in his art. It serves as a reminder that art can be a powerful tool for exploring and understanding the world around us.

Although the mural was never completed, the Battle of Anghiari project remains an important part of Leonardo's legacy, showcasing his innovative thinking and his revolutionary approach to art and science.

Leonardo's exploration of military engineering and his study of human anatomy in relation to motion have significantly influenced the way art is created and perceived today. His dedication to understanding the human body and his commitment to capturing its dynamic nature continue to inspire artists and scientists alike.

MARK LYLANI

The Mona Lisa

The Mona Lisa is one of Leonardo da Vinci's most famous paintings and is considered a masterpiece of the Renaissance period. The painting is also known as La Gioconda, which means "the joyful one" in Italian. It was created between 1503 and 1506, during Leonardo's time in Florence.

This portrait depicts a woman named Lisa Gherardini, believed to be the wife of a Florentine merchant named Francesco del Giocondo. The identity of the sitter has not been definitively proven, but Lisa Gherardini is a popular theory. The painting captures her enigmatic smile and has intrigued people for centuries.

Leonardo experimented with a technique called sfumato, which involves gently blending colors and tones to create soft edges and a sense of depth. This technique gives the painting a realistic and lifelike quality.

One of the reasons the Mona Lisa is so famous is because of its mysterious history. It has been a part of the Louvre's collection, but it did gain international attention after it was stolen in 1911. The painting was missing for over two years and was eventually recovered and returned to the museum.

Another reason for its fame is the subject's enigmatic smile. Many art lovers and experts have debated the meaning behind her smile. Some believe it reflects different emotions, while others think it represents the sitter's subtle and complex nature.

In addition to the smile, Leonardo paid great attention to the details of the painting. He meticulously painted the texture of the skin, the folds of the clothing, and the play of light on various surfaces.

The Mona Lisa is painted on a small wood panel, measuring only approximately 30 x 21 inches. Despite its small size, the painting has attracted millions of viewers from around the world, who come to see it at the Louvre Museum in Paris.

Leonardo worked on the painting for many years, but it is not accurate to say that he carried it with him wherever he traveled. He did consider it unfinished and always strived for perfection. He believed that art was never truly complete, and he continually experimented with different techniques and styles.

The Mona Lisa is now regarded as one of the most famous paintings in the world and is an iconic symbol of art history. Its combination of technical innovation, mysterious subject, and Leonardo's skillful execution continues to captivate audiences of all ages.

Engineering and Inventions

Leonardo da Vinci was not only a skilled artist, but he was also a brilliant engineer and inventor. His curiosity and imagination led him to explore various fields of study, including mechanics, hydraulics, and aerodynamics. Throughout his lifetime, Leonardo designed numerous machines and inventions that were far ahead of his time.

One of his most famous engineering projects was his design for a flying machine. Leonardo was fascinated with the idea of human flight and spent years studying birds and their wings. He sketched out plans for a gadget that would allow a person to soar through the air. Although he never built a working flying machine, his designs and ideas laid the foundation for future aviation pioneers.

Leonardo also had a keen interest in engineering projects that aimed to make life easier. He invented several machines, such as a bicycle-like contraption that was powered by the rider's feet and hands. He even designed a self-propelled cart, which is considered an early prototype for the modern automobile.

One of Leonardo's most innovative inventions was the concept of a diving suit. He recognized the potential for humans to explore the depths of the sea and came up with a design for a suit that would allow them to breathe underwater. His diving suit had a helmet-like structure connected to a tube for air supply. While the technology of his time did not allow for the construction of a functional diving suit, his ideas paved the way for future advancements in underwater exploration.

Leonardo was also fascinated by the power of water and its ability to generate energy. He designed various water-powered machines, including mills and pumps, which utilized the force of moving water to perform tasks. His designs for dams and canals showcased his understanding of hydraulics and water management.

In addition to his engineering projects, Leonardo was known for his innovative military inventions. He designed fortified structures, cannons, and even a vehicle with armored plating. His military designs were often focused on enhancing defense strategies and creating more efficient weapons.

Throughout his life, Leonardo kept detailed

sketches and notes about his inventions, filling his notebooks with ideas and concepts. His drawings showed intricate details and precise measurements, demonstrating his meticulous approach to engineering. While many of his inventions were never built during his lifetime, his forward-thinking ideas and designs continue to inspire scientists, engineers, and inventors to this day. Leonardo da Vinci truly was a Renaissance man, contributing greatly to both the arts and the sciences.

Later Years in Milan

In his later years, Leonardo da Vinci continued his artistic and scientific endeavors as he returned to Milan, an important city in Italy during the Renaissance period. He was welcomed back to the city with open arms, and his reputation as a brilliant artist and an intellectual genius grew even stronger.

Leonardo received numerous commissions from powerful patrons, including Ludovico Sforza, the Duke of Milan. One of his most important works during this time was the bronze equestrian statue of the duke's father, Francesco Sforza. Unfortunately, due to a shortage of bronze, the statue was never completed, and the metal was eventually used for weapons in times of war.

During his time in Milan, Leonardo also dedicated himself to studying anatomy. He performed dissections on human corpses, which he believed were essential to understanding the human body and improving his art. His detailed anatomical drawings and observations paved the way for future advancements in medical science.

Among his other artistic achievements, Leonardo painted the beautiful portrait of Cecilia Gallerani, known as "The Lady with an Ermine." This painting showcased Leonardo's skills in capturing the essence of his subjects, using light and shadow to bring them to life on the canvas.

Leonardo's interest in engineering and invention continued in Milan as well. He worked on designs for flying machines, submarines, and even a mechanical lion that could walk and function autonomously. Although many of his inventions remained merely as sketches and models, they demonstrated Leonardo's incredible imagination and innovative thinking.

Leonardo's years in Milan were marked by his insatiable curiosity and thirst for knowledge. He constantly carried around a notebook, filling its pages with his observations, ideas, and sketches. These notebooks, known as his "Codices," contain a wealth of knowledge on a wide range of subjects, from art and anatomy to engineering and mathematics.

Leonardo's departure from Milan came when French forces invaded the city. He then embarked on a different chapter in his life, moving to Rome. However, his time in Milan had a lasting impact on both his art and scientific pursuits.

Leonardo's later years in Milan were filled with artistic masterpieces, scientific discoveries, and groundbreaking inventions. His time in this vibrant city allowed him to expand his knowledge and further shape the Renaissance era with his unique talents and ideas.

Work in Rome

After spending several years in Milan, Leonardo da Vinci received an invitation from Giuliano de' Medici to come and work in Rome. Giuliano was known for being a great patron of the arts, and he wanted Leonardo to help beautify the city with his talents.

Leonardo arrived in Rome in the year 1513 and immediately began working on various projects for the Pope. One of his most famous works during this time was a painting called "The Virgin and Child with Saint Anne." This painting showcased Leonardo's incredible attention to detail and his skill in capturing human emotions.

In addition to his paintings, Leonardo also worked on designs for buildings, including a project to rebuild the Church of San Giovanni dei Fiorentini. He created detailed plans for the church's facade and interior, but unfortunately, the project was never realized.

Leonardo's time in Rome was not without challenges. There were conflicts and power struggles within the city, which at times interfered with his work. Despite these difficulties, Leonardo managed to create a number of remarkable drawings and scientific studies during his stay.

One of Leonardo's most notable achievements in Rome was his collaboration with the famous architect Donato Bramante. They worked on designing the Belvedere Courtyard in the Vatican Palace. Their vision for the courtyard incorporated classical elements of ancient Roman architecture, creating a harmonious blend of beauty and functionality.

During his years in Rome, Leonardo also continued his scientific investigations. He conducted experiments with water and studied the movement of rivers. He was fascinated by the way water flowed and how it could be harnessed for various purposes. Leonardo's findings in this area would later contribute to advancements in engineering and hydrodynamics.

Although Leonardo spent only a few years in Rome, his impact on the city was significant. His artistic and architectural contributions influenced generations of artists and architects to come. His scientific studies and experiments laid the groundwork for future discoveries. Even today, Leonardo's presence can be felt in the art and architecture of Rome.

As Leonardo left Rome and moved on to new adventures, he continued to push the boundaries of art and science. His insatiable curiosity and endless creativity made him one of history's most remarkable individuals.

Architectural Designs

Leonardo da Vinci was not just a talented artist and scientist, but he was also a brilliant architect. In this chapter, we will explore some of his architectural designs that are still admired and studied today.

One of Leonardo's most famous architectural designs is the plan for the ideal city of Imola. He carefully sketched out every detail, showing streets, buildings, and even a central square. His design incorporated elements of symmetry and harmony, creating a city that was not just functional but also beautiful to look at. Although Imola was never built exactly as

Leonardo envisioned, his design inspired many future architects.

Another impressive architectural design by Leonardo was the scheme he created for the Palace of Piombino. This design was made for the Italian nobleman Cesare Borgia. Leonardo's plan included a grand entrance, large courtyards, and a stunning central hall. Unfortunately, this design was never realized, but it showcased Leonardo's talent for creating grand and elegant structures.

Leonardo also had plans for a cathedral in Milan. His design included a huge central dome that would have been taller than any other in Europe at the time. Leonardo's innovative ideas included using numerous smaller domes to support the central one, preventing it from collapsing. Although his design was never built, it influenced later architects who constructed impressive domes, such as the one of St. Peter's Basilica in Rome.

In addition to creating new architectural designs, Leonardo also worked on renovating existing buildings. One example of this is the proposed renovation of the Church of San Francesco in Milan. Leonardo's plan aimed to transform the church into a grand mausoleum for the Sforza family, who were the ruling family of Milan. His design included ornate tombs and beautifully decorated walls. Unfortunately, financial difficulties prevented the completion of the project, and Leonardo's designs remained on paper.

One of Leonardo's most ambitious

architectural projects was the plan for a new city at the mouth of the Arno River. The city was intended to be a trading hub and a military stronghold. Leonardo's design included a series of fortresses, a system of canals for transportation, and even a spiral staircase for the central tower. However, like many of his architectural designs, this project never came to fruition.

Leonardo's architectural designs were truly ahead of their time. He combined his artistic skills with his scientific knowledge to create innovative and beautiful structures. Although many of his designs were never built, they continue to inspire and captivate architects and artists to this day.

Move to France

After spending many years traveling and working in various cities, Leonardo decided to settle down in Amboise, a small town in France, during the final years of his life. He was already in his sixties, but his passion for learning and creating had not diminished.

Leonardo was invited to Amboise by King Francis I, who was a great admirer of his work. The king provided Leonardo with a mansion called the Clos Lucé, which was located near the royal residence at Château d'Amboise. Leonardo was given the title of "First Painter, Engineer, and Architect to the King."

Even though he was officially retired, Leonardo continued to work on his artistic and scientific projects. He spent his time studying and experimenting, filling his notebooks with observations, sketches, and ideas. He also wrote letters to his friends and patrons, sharing his thoughts and discoveries.

During this time, Leonardo focused more on his scientific studies rather than painting. He delved deeper into his investigations of anatomy, botany, geology, and engineering. He studied human bodies to understand the intricacies of the human form and made detailed drawings of various organs.

Leonardo continued to create magnificent artwork as well. One of his last paintings, called "Saint John the Baptist," showcased his mastery of light and shadow. The painting portrays Saint John with expressive eyes and a captivating smile.

Although Leonardo had his hands occupied with his own projects, he also provided advice and guidance to other artists who visited him at the Clos Lucé. His opinions were highly respected, and young artists sought his wisdom on matters of art and design.

In his final years, Leonardo also had the opportunity to meet and converse with other great thinkers and artists of the time, such as the renowned Renaissance artist Raphael. These intellectual exchanges fueled his creativity and allowed him to expand his knowledge even further.

Sadly, Leonardo da Vinci passed away on May 2, 1519, at the age of 67. His death was a great loss to the world of art and science. He was buried in the Chapel of Saint Hubert in Château d'Amboise.

Even though Leonardo's life had come to an end, his legacy lived on. His extraordinary contributions to both art and science would influence generations to come. His notebooks, filled with his thoughts and observations, were rediscovered centuries later and shed further light on his genius.

The Clos Lucé is now a museum dedicated to Leonardo da Vinci's life and work. Visitors can explore his former residence and see replicas of his inventions and artworks. The museum stands as a tribute to the incredible mind and imagination of Leonardo da Vinci, one of the greatest geniuses in history.

Leonardo's Legacy

Leonardo da Vinci was a remarkable artist, inventor, scientist, and engineer. His contributions continue to inspire and impact the world, even today.

One of Leonardo's greatest contributions was his extensive study of the human body. He believed that understanding human anatomy was crucial for creating accurate and lifelike art. Leonardo's anatomical studies were meticulous and detailed, providing valuable insights. His sketches of muscles, bones, and organs continue to be used by medical students and professionals to this day, expanding our knowledge of the human body's inner workings.

Leonardo's curiosity and innovative mind also led him to create numerous inventions. Although many of these ideas were far ahead of his time, such as flying machines and armored vehicles, they demonstrated Leonardo's imagination and foresight.

One of Leonardo's notable inventions was his design for a mechanical knight, also known as an automaton. This robotic-like figure had the ability to move and perform actions on its own. While he never built a working automaton, his ideas laid the foundation for future advancements in robotics.

In addition to his scientific and engineering pursuits, Leonardo's artistic style greatly influenced the Renaissance and subsequent art movements. He revolutionized the use of perspective, realistic depiction of nature, and mastery of light and shadow, setting himself apart from his contemporaries.

Arguably, Leonardo's most famous painting, the Mona Lisa, continues to captivate audiences with its enigmatic smile. This masterpiece showcases his exceptional skills in creating a sense of depth and emotion in his subjects.

Leonardo's legacy extends beyond his individual works. His ideas and methods continue to inspire new generations of artists, scientists, and inventors. His emphasis on observation, experimentation, and learning from nature serves as a valuable lesson for anyone seeking to explore new frontiers.

As time went on, Leonardo's notebooks were discovered, revealing the depth of his knowledge and ideas. His fascination with flight, anatomy, and engineering reflect a curious mind always seeking to understand the world around him.

Leonardo's influence can also be seen in popular culture today. His image and works are often referenced in movies, books, and various forms of media. He has become an enduring symbol of genius and creativity, inspiring countless artists and thinkers.

So, as we reflect on the life and work of Leonardo da Vinci, we can truly appreciate the incredible legacy he left behind. His art, inventions, and scientific studies continue to shape our understanding of the world. Leonardo's insatiable curiosity and relentless pursuit of knowledge serve as an inspiration for us all.

Rediscovery of Notebooks

During the long span of time after Leonardo da Vinci's death, his notebooks were scattered and forgotten. For centuries, these precious pages remained hidden until a remarkable discovery brought them back to light.

In 1891, a historian named Giovanni Poggiali discovered a collection of Leonardo's notes and sketches in the Biblioteca Ambrosiana, a library in Milan, Italy. The set of notebooks, now known as the Codex Atlanticus, included around 1,200 pages filled with Leonardo's observations, ideas, and drawings on a variety of subjects.

Thanks to the rediscovery of these notebooks, we gained a deeper understanding of Leonardo's genius.

The Codex Atlanticus contained sections dedicated to engineering, science, mathematics, anatomy, architecture, and even music. Within its pages, Leonardo explored everything from the flight of birds to the human circulatory system, from the design of war machines to the creation of beautiful paintings.

The notebooks were written in Leonardo's characteristic "mirror writing," where the text is written in reverse and can only be read by holding it up to a mirror. This unique writing style ensured that Leonardo's thoughts and ideas would remain private during his lifetime.

As the notebooks were rediscovered, scholars and scientists pored over their contents, deciphering the text and marveling at the depth of Leonardo's knowledge. They discovered his meticulous observation of the natural world and his innovative ideas that were ahead of his time. Leonardo's notebooks revealed his fascination with the human body as he conducted detailed anatomical studies. He dissected corpses to gain a better understanding of the body's inner workings, creating accurate illustrations that are still admired today.

The notebooks also demonstrated Leonardo's innovative engineering designs. His drawings of flying machines, bridges, and military weapons showed his ability to combine art and science. He even envisioned machines that could harness the power of nature, such as a device to control the flow of rivers.

The rediscovery of Leonardo's notebooks not only provided a deeper insight into his genius but also inspired generations of scientists, artists, and inventors. Many of his ideas, such as the concept of a helicopter or a diving suit, became the precursors for inventions that are still in use today.

In 1965, the Codex Leicester, another one of Leonardo's notebooks, was purchased by an American billionaire named Armand Hammer. It contains Leonardo's extensive notes and sketches on numerous scientific topics, particularly his observations on water and its properties. The Codex Leicester remains one of the most expensive books ever sold.

Today, Leonardo's notebooks are treasured possessions housed in museums and libraries around the world. They serve as a testament to his insatiable curiosity and his relentless pursuit of knowledge.

The rediscovery of these notebooks not only gave us a glimpse into the mind of one of history's greatest geniuses, but it also reminds us of the importance of recording our thoughts, ideas, and observations. Who knows? Perhaps the notebooks of future generations hold the key to unlocking even more remarkable discoveries.

MARK LYLANI

Leonardo in Popular Culture

Leonardo da Vinci was not just an incredible artist and scientist during his lifetime, but his legacy continues to inspire and captivate people today, including popular culture. From books and movies to artwork and advertising, Leonardo's influence can be seen in various aspects of modern society.

One of the most famous examples of Leonardo's presence in popular culture is his portrayal in Dan Brown's bestselling novel, "The Da Vinci Code." This thrilling story combines art, history, and mystery, with Leonardo's art playing a central role in deciphering codes and solving puzzles.

Leonardo's masterpiece, the Mona Lisa, is another prime example of his lasting impact on popular culture. With her enigmatic smile, the Mona Lisa has been recreated, parodied, and referenced in countless works of art, cartoons, and advertisements. Her image can be found on everything from t-shirts to coffee mugs!

Leonardo's inventions and engineering drawings have also made their way into popular culture. From puzzles and models inspired by his designs to video games and animated movies, his concepts for flying machines, war machines, and futuristic inventions have sparked the imagination of both young and old.

Leonardo's notebooks, filled with his scientific observations and sketches, have also become a popular subject in literature and art. Books such as "Leonardo's

Notebooks" by H. Anna Suh provide a glimpse into the mind of this genius and inspire young readers to explore their own creativity and curiosity.

In the world of film, Leonardo has been portrayed by various actors, bringing his character to life on the big screen. One notable example is the 2006 film "The Genius Club," where Leonardo is depicted as one of history's greatest geniuses, called upon to contribute to solving a global crisis.

Throughout the years, museums and galleries have hosted exhibitions dedicated to Leonardo's work, allowing people to experience his art firsthand. These exhibitions often include interactive displays and multimedia presentations, making his inventions and artwork accessible to people of all ages.

Leonardo's influence on popular culture goes beyond books and movies. His art techniques and innovative ideas have inspired artists, scientists, and inventors throughout history. From the masterpieces of other Renaissance painters to the futuristic designs of modern architects, Leonardo's impact can be seen in many artistic and scientific fields.

Leonardo continues to be a source of fascination and inspiration to people around the world. His work and ideas transcend time and continue to be celebrated and admired today. By exploring Leonardo's legacy in popular culture, we can gain a deeper appreciation for the genius and creativity of this remarkable man.

Famous Quotes and Sayings

Have you ever heard a famous saying or quote that has stuck with you? Well, Leonardo da Vinci had a way with words, too. Let's take a look at some of his most famous quotes and what they mean.

One of Leonardo's most well-known quotes is, "Simplicity is the ultimate sophistication." This means that simplicity is not just about being basic or plain, but it is about finding beauty and elegance in simplicity.

Leonardo believed that simplicity could be

found in nature and art. Sometimes, the most simple things can be the most beautiful.

Another famous quote by Leonardo is, "Art is never finished, only abandoned." This quote emphasizes Leonardo's belief that an artist's work is never truly finished. Even when a painting or sculpture is complete, there is always room for improvement and refinement. Leonardo believed that art is a constant process of learning and growing and that an artist should always strive to become better.

Leonardo also said, "Learning never exhausts the mind." This quote highlights Leonardo's belief in the power of continuous learning. He believed that the mind has an unlimited capacity to gain knowledge and that learning is a lifelong journey. Leonardo's own curiosity and thirst for knowledge led him to explore various fields of study, from art and science to engineering and anatomy.

In addition, Leonardo said, "Realize that everything connects to everything else." This quote highlights Leonardo's fascination with the interconnectedness of the world. He believed that everything in nature, from plants and animals to rivers and mountains, is connected in some way. Leonardo encouraged people to observe and understand these connections, as it would lead to a deeper understanding of the world.

Furthermore, Leonardo said, "It had long since come to my attention that people of accomplishment rarely sat back and let things happen to them. They went out and happened to things." This quote shows Leonardo's belief in taking action and making things happen. He believed that successful people are not passive, but rather, they actively pursue their goals and dreams. Leonardo himself was a perfect example of this, as he was always working on new inventions, making discoveries, and creating art.

Lastly, Leonardo said, "Where the spirit does not work with the hand, there is no art." This quote emphasizes the importance of passion and creativity in art. Leonardo believed that true art comes from the heart and soul and that technical skill alone is not enough. An artist must have a deep connection to their work and infuse it with their own spirit and emotions.

These were just a few of the many inspiring

and insightful quotes by Leonardo da Vinci. Leonardo's words continue to resonate with people even today because they capture the essence of his genius and his philosophy on life and art. So, the next time you come across a famous quote or saying, remember that there is often a deeper meaning behind it. Just like Leonardo, take the time to reflect on the words and apply them to your own life. Who knows, you might be inspired to create something amazing, just like Leonardo da Vinci.

MARK LYLANI

Myths and Misconceptions

Leonardo da Vinci was a remarkable artist, scientist, and inventor whose genius has captivated the world for centuries. However, over time, many myths and misconceptions have formed about his life and work. Let's shine a light on some of these misconceptions and separate fact from fiction.

Myth 1: Leonardo was the archetype of the "starving artist."

Contrary to popular belief, Leonardo was not a "starving artist." In fact, he was incredibly wealthy, thanks to his successful career and the patronage of powerful individuals like the Duke of Milan. He earned a significant income from his commissions and had a steady source of income throughout his life.

Myth 2: Leonardo was a loner.

While Leonardo did spend a considerable amount of time working alone in his studio, he was far from being a recluse. He had a wide circle of friends and acquaintances, including other artists, scientists, and scholars. He enjoyed their company and actively sought collaboration and intellectual exchange.

Myth 3: Leonardo only painted the Mona Lisa and The Last Supper.

While the Mona Lisa and The Last Supper are two of Leonardo's most famous works, they are just a small fraction of his artistic output. Leonardo created numerous breathtaking paintings, drawings, and sculptures throughout his career. Some of his notable works include The Baptism of Christ, The Virgin and Child with Saint Anne, and The Annunciation.

Myth 4: Leonardo was a time-traveler or possessed supernatural powers.

As incredible as Leonardo's achievements were, he was not a time traveler or possessed any supernatural powers. His accomplishments can be attributed to his extraordinary intellect, keen observation skills, and relentless curiosity. Leonardo studied the world around him and used his imagination to explore new ideas and possibilities, but he was very much a product of his time.

Myth 5: Leonardo was a sloppy and unreliable worker.

On the contrary, Leonardo was known for his meticulous attention to detail and his unwavering commitment to excellence. He would spend countless hours perfecting his artworks, experimenting with different techniques, and refining his scientific discoveries. Leonardo's dedication to his craft is evident in the intricate details and flawless execution of his works.

Myth 6: Leonardo's inventions were all failures.

While not all of Leonardo's inventions were successful, many of his designs were groundbreaking and ahead of their time. Leonardo conceptualized ideas for flying machines, war machines, and even a submarine. Although some of his inventions were never built during his lifetime due to technological limitations, they laid the foundation for future advancements in science and engineering.

Myth 7: Leonardo died a forgotten and unappreciated artist.

Contrary to this myth, Leonardo's work was highly regarded during his lifetime. He received commissions from esteemed patrons, such as the Pope and French King Francis I. His notebooks and artworks were collected and studied by other artists and scientists even after his death. His reputation as a genius persisted long after he passed away, and his influence on art and science continues to this day.

By dispelling these myths and misconceptions, we gain a clearer and more accurate understanding of Leonardo da Vinci's extraordinary life and contributions. He was not only a true visionary but also a man of great talent and intellect who forever changed the world with his brilliance.

Fun Facts about Leonardo

Leonardo da Vinci was not only a brilliant artist and inventor, but he was also a fascinating individual with many interesting facts surrounding his life and work. In this chapter, we will uncover some fun and surprising facts about Leonardo that will amaze you.

Fact 1: Leonardo was an excellent musician. He was skilled in playing the lyre and was often asked to perform at various social gatherings. Music was a significant part of his life, and he believed it had the power to heal and bring joy to people.

Fact 2: Leonardo had a deep love for nature and animals. He would often visit the countryside to observe birds, insects, and plants, meticulously studying them and recording his observations in his famous notebooks. His detailed illustrations of plants and animals were an important contribution to the scientific understanding of the natural world.

Fact 3: Leonardo was ambidextrous, meaning he could use both his right and left hands with equal ease. This ability was incredibly useful for his artistic work, as he could sketch, paint, and write with either hand. It is believed that his ambidexterity enhanced his observational skills and allowed him to depict the human body more accurately.

Fact 4: Leonardo had a habit of buying caged birds in order to set them free. He believed that all creatures had the right to be free and enjoy their lives in their natural habitats. This act of kindness towards animals demonstrated his compassionate nature.

Fact 5: Despite being renowned for his artistic talent, Leonardo struggled with completing many of his works. He was a perfectionist and would often abandon his paintings, feeling dissatisfied with the result. This tendency to leave projects unfinished has left art historians with only a limited number of Leonardo's completed artworks.

Fact 6: Leonardo's curiosity knew no bounds, and he constantly sought to explore and understand the world around him. He would spend hours dissecting human bodies to study anatomy, dissecting animals to understand their internal structures, and conducting experiments to unravel the mysteries of flight.

Fact 7: Leonardo was an avid thinker and observer of human behavior. He would often sit in public places, sketchbook in hand, observing people's facial expressions, gestures, and body language. These observations helped him capture the essence of human emotion and movement in his artwork.

Fact 8: Leonardo had a fascination with water and hydraulics. He designed innovative water systems, including canals and aqueducts, and even invented a diving suit. His understanding of water dynamics greatly influenced his engineering projects and artistic depictions of water.

Fact 9: Leonardo was a vegetarian, which was a rare choice during his time. He believed in the importance of respecting all living creatures and promoting a balanced and harmonious relationship with nature. His vegetarian lifestyle was reflective of his values and philosophies.

Fact 10: Leonardo's notebooks were not just filled with sketches and scientific observations but also with his thoughts, ideas, and reflections. These personal notebooks, known as "codices," provide a glimpse into the mind of a true Renaissance genius, offering insights into both his artistic and scientific thinking.

These fascinating facts about Leonardo da Vinci give us a deeper understanding of the man behind the masterpieces. His artistic talent, scientific curiosity, and compassionate nature continue to inspire and captivate people of all ages.

MARK LYLANI

Tools and Techniques

Leonardo da Vinci was not only a talented artist and inventor but also a master of various tools and techniques. His curiosity and innovative thinking led him to explore new ways of creating art and conducting scientific studies. In this chapter, we will uncover some of the tools and techniques Leonardo used during his remarkable career.

One of Leonardo's most famous techniques was sfumato, which means "smoky" in Italian. He used this technique to create soft, hazy transitions between colors and tones. By blending colors together, he achieved a realistic and mysterious effect in his paintings. This technique can be seen in his masterpiece, the Mona Lisa.

Leonardo also perfected the art of chiaroscuro, which refers to the contrasting play of light and shadow. By skillfully using light and dark shades, he added depth and volume to his artworks. This technique can be observed in his famous painting, The Last Supper, where the dramatic interplay of light and shadow brings the figures to life.

An essential tool in Leonardo's artistic arsenal was the paintbrush. However, he didn't limit himself to conventional brushes. He experimented with different sizes and shapes, including rounded and flat brushes, to achieve different effects in his paintings. He would combine various brushstrokes to create texture and detail in his artwork.

In addition to traditional painting tools,

Leonardo also utilized technology and innovation. He invented his own silverpoint stylus for drawing. This pencil-like instrument had a silver tip, which, when applied to specially prepared paper, created lines with remarkable precision and fine detail.

Leonardo's notebooks reveal his fascination with scientific observation and his meticulous nature. He frequently used red chalk to make accurate sketches and annotations, capturing his observations of anatomy, nature, and physics. His use of red chalk allowed him to emphasize key details and give his drawings a distinctive look.

Besides painting and drawing tools, Leonardo also employed various materials for his artistic creations. He experimented with different types of pigments and binders to create vibrant and long-lasting colors. Some of the materials he used included natural pigments derived from minerals, plants, and even insects. His use of these materials contributed to the richness and durability of his artworks.

Leonardo's commitment to innovation extended beyond his artistic endeavors. He was fascinated by the potential of technology and engineering. To aid his scientific and anatomical studies, he developed his own lens grinders, creating high-quality lenses that allowed him to observe the world in detail. He also tinkered with mirrors and constructed models to study the principles of light and reflection.

In conclusion, Leonardo da Vinci's tools and techniques played a crucial role in shaping his artistic and scientific achievements. His mastery of sfumato, chiaroscuro, and innovative use of brushes, pencils, and materials revolutionized the art world. By combining his artistic skills with his scientific knowledge, Leonardo left a lasting legacy that continues to inspire artists and inventors to this day.

MARK LYLANI

Influence on Modern Science

Leonardo da Vinci was not only a talented artist but also a brilliant scientist and inventor. His observations and ideas have had a profound impact on modern science. Let's explore some of the ways Leonardo's work still influences our understanding of the world today.

One of Leonardo's notable contributions to modern science is his study of anatomy. He wanted to understand the human body in great detail, so he dissected cadavers. Through careful examination, he made important discoveries about the inner workings of the human body. Leonardo's detailed drawings of muscles, bones, and organs have provided valuable insights to anatomists for centuries. His work in anatomy continues to be studied and referenced by scientists and medical professionals to advance our understanding of the human body.

Leonardo was also fascinated by the natural world and its phenomena. He studied and documented various subjects, such as the flight of birds, the movement of water, and the growth of plants. His observations on these subjects laid the foundation for the fields of aerodynamics, hydrodynamics, and botany. Today, scientists still refer to Leonardo's notes and drawings when exploring these areas of study. His keen observations and curiosity sparked new ways of thinking about the natural world and continue to inspire scientific discoveries.

One of Leonardo's most famous ideas for an invention was the "ornithopter," a flying machine based on his observations of bird flight. The design incorporated flapping wings inspired by how birds soar through the air. While Leonardo's ornithopter was never built during his lifetime, his principles greatly influenced the development of aviation. Today, engineers and scientists continue to look to Leonardo's work for inspiration when designing new aircraft and exploring the possibilities of flight. His innovative ideas helped pave the way for human flight.

Leonardo's curiosity extended to the field of engineering as well. He invented a wide range of devices, including a revolving bridge, portable bridges, and even a diving suit. Some of his ideas were far ahead of his time and have influenced modern technology. For example, Leonardo's concepts of a self-propelled cart and automated machines became a reality in the form of automobiles and advanced robotics that we see today. His inventions and engineering concepts demonstrate his innovative thinking and have shaped the world we live in.

In addition to his scientific and engineering pursuits, Leonardo also made significant contributions to mathematics. He studied geometry and perspective to create realistic and accurate representations in his artwork. Leonardo's understanding of these mathematical principles influenced many other artists and architects of the Renaissance period. His approach to applying mathematical concepts to art helped bring a sense of realism and proportion to artistic creations.

Leonardo da Vinci's influence on modern science cannot be overstated. His meticulous observations, innovative ideas, and groundbreaking inventions have shaped the way we understand and interact with the world. Scientists, engineers, and artists continue to draw inspiration from his work, proving that Leonardo's genius transcends time and continues to be relevant in the modern age. As you explore the world around you, remember the curious and creative spirit of Leonardo da Vinci. Who knows, maybe you will make a discovery or invent something amazing too!

MARK LYLANI

Patronage and Commissions

Leonardo da Vinci's incredible artistic talents attracted the attention of many powerful and wealthy individuals during the Renaissance. These patrons recognized Leonardo's genius and were eager to commission his artworks. A commission is a request for a piece of art to be created specifically for a person or group.

One of Leonardo's first important patrons was Ludovico Sforza, the Duke of Milan. He admired Leonardo's work and hired him to create various pieces, including paintings, sculptures, and even elaborate stage sets for parties and events. Leonardo spent nearly 20 years in Milan, working on several important commissions for the Duke.

One of the most famous commissions during this time was "The Last Supper." The Duke asked Leonardo to paint a mural depicting the biblical event of Jesus sharing his final meal with his disciples. Leonardo painstakingly worked on this masterpiece for several years, using a new technique that had the unintended consequence of leading to the painting's deterioration. Despite this, "The Last Supper" remains one of the most iconic works of art in history.

Another prominent patron of Leonardo was Cesare Borgia, a powerful political figure and military leader. Borgia hired Leonardo as a military architect and engineer, relying on his expertise to design fortresses and weapons. Leonardo created detailed plans and sketches for war machines, such as tanks and cannons. Although these inventions were not built during Leonardo's time, his ideas greatly influenced future military technology.

Leonardo also received commissions from the Catholic Church. He was asked to create religious artworks for churches and monasteries. One of his notable works is the "Virgin of the Rocks," a painting depicting the Virgin Mary and baby Jesus. It is believed that Leonardo started this commission in Milan but completed it later when he returned to Florence.

In addition to individuals and institutions, Leonardo pursued his own artistic ideas and created self-commissioned works. He was fascinated by anatomy and human proportions, and he set out to create a new kind of artwork called "The Adoration of the

Magi." This painting was intended to showcase his knowledge and understanding of anatomy by depicting figures in various poses and perspectives. Unfortunately, Leonardo never finished this painting, leaving it as an unfinished masterpiece.

Leonardo's commissions and patronage relationships allowed him to explore his artistic talents and pursue his passion for knowledge. His artwork and inventions fascinated the world and left a lasting impact on the art and science of future generations.

Artistic Style

Leonardo da Vinci was a true master when it came to art. He had a unique style that set him apart from other artists of his time.

Leonardo was known for his use of perspective, which is a technique that creates the illusion of depth and distance in a painting. He was able to create lifelike scenes by carefully observing how objects diminish in size as they move into the distance. One of his most famous paintings, "The Last Supper," demonstrates his mastery of perspective as the figures in the painting appear to recede into the background.

Another characteristic of Leonardo's artistic style was his attention to detail. He was known to spend hours studying and sketching his subjects before even beginning to paint. He believed that a true artist must have a deep understanding of the world around them in order to represent it in their art accurately.

Leonardo's paintings were also known for their softness and blending of colors. He used a technique called sfumato, which involves softly smoothing and blending colors to create a seamless transition. This technique gives his paintings a sense of depth and realism.

In addition to his technical skills, Leonardo was also adept at capturing emotion and expression in his paintings. He believed that art should not only be beautiful but should also evoke feelings in the viewer. One of the best examples of this is his famous painting, the "Mona Lisa." The painting's enigmatic smile is said to captivate viewers and leave them wondering about the subject's thoughts and emotions.

Leonardo was also known for his use of light and shadow in his paintings. He carefully observed how light falls on different objects and used this knowledge to create realistic and three-dimensional effects. This technique, known as chiaroscuro, gives his paintings a sense of depth and drama.

Throughout his career, Leonardo da Vinci experimented with different mediums and techniques. He was not just a painter but also a sculptor, architect, and engineer. He constantly pushed the boundaries of art, exploring new ways to represent the world around him.

Leonardo's artistic style was truly groundbreaking and continues to be admired and studied by artists today. His attention to detail, use of perspective, mastery of color and light, and ability to capture emotion make him one of the greatest artists of all time.

Contributions to the Renaissance

Leonardo da Vinci made numerous significant contributions to the Renaissance movement. His abilities as an artist, scientist, and engineer helped shape the world we live in today.

One of Leonardo's most notable contributions was his ability to combine art and science. He believed that a true artist should have a deep understanding of the natural world. Leonardo's meticulous observations and detailed anatomical studies allowed him to accurately depict the human body in his artwork, creating a newfound realism in the art world.

Leonardo also made important advancements in the field of engineering. His innovative ideas for inventions and machines were far ahead of his time. Some of his designs, such as the flying machine and the armored tank, were visionary and displayed his creative thinking.

In addition to his artwork and engineering projects, Leonardo's notebooks reveal his interest in many scientific fields. He conducted experiments and made observations in various areas, including anatomy, astronomy, botany, and geology. His curiosity and thirst for knowledge were instrumental in advancing scientific understanding during the Renaissance.

Leonardo's artistic style, characterized by soft shading, atmospheric perspective, and lifelike representations of human emotions, greatly influenced other artists of the time.

Many artists were inspired by his techniques, such as sfumato (blurring or softening of edges), and incorporated them into their own works.

Leonardo's patronage and commissions from wealthy and influential individuals allowed him to pursue his artistic endeavors. He had the opportunity to create masterpieces for patrons such as the Duke of Milan and the Medici family. This support enabled him to focus on his art and develop his unique style.

Another contribution of Leonardo to the Renaissance was his emphasis on the importance of observation and the use of empirical evidence. He believed that true knowledge could only be obtained through direct observation and experimentation. Leonardo's approach to learning paved the way for the scientific method we rely on today.

Leonardo's impact on the Renaissance was not limited to his own time. His notebooks, filled with sketches, ideas, and scientific observations, were rediscovered centuries after his death. They continue to inspire and fascinate scientists, artists, and inventors.

In summary, Leonardo da Vinci made significant contributions to the Renaissance movement through his integration of art and science, his innovative engineering designs, his scientific observations, and his influence on other artists. His legacy remains influential to this day, as his ideas continue to shape and inspire the fields of art and science.

Summary and Reflection

Now that we have learned about the incredible life and accomplishments of Leonardo da Vinci, let's take a moment to summarize and reflect on everything we have discovered about this brilliant artist, scientist, and inventor.

Leonardo was born in Vinci, Italy, in 1452. He showed great talent and curiosity from an early age, and his artistic abilities led him to become an apprentice to the famous artist Andrea del Verrocchio. During his apprenticeship, Leonardo learned various techniques and honed his skills.

As he developed as an artist, Leonardo created some amazing early works, including "The Baptism of Christ" and "Annunciation." These paintings demonstrated his exceptional attention to detail and his ability to capture human emotions.

In 1482, Leonardo moved to Milan, where he received several important commissions. One of his most famous works, "The Last Supper," was completed during this time. Leonardo's ability to capture the expressions of the disciples and the dramatic moment of the Last Supper made this painting a masterpiece.

However, Leonardo's interests were not limited to art. He was fascinated by science and anatomy. He conducted in-depth studies of the human body, creating detailed drawings and diagrams of the human anatomy. His illustrations provided insights into how the human body functions.

In 1503, Leonardo returned to Florence, where he worked on various projects, including the famous "Mona Lisa." This mysterious painting, with its enigmatic smile, has captivated people for centuries. It is considered one of the greatest pieces of art in history.

Leonardo's engineering and inventions were truly ahead of his time. He developed designs for flying machines, submarines, and even a robotic knight. Although many of his ideas were never built, they demonstrated his innovative thinking and his desire to push the boundaries of knowledge.

During his later years, Leonardo continued to work in Milan and then in Rome. He left behind an impressive collection of architectural designs, showcasing his vision for grand buildings and cities. His ideas were often revolutionary, incorporating innovative concepts and aesthetic beauty.

Leonardo eventually moved to France, where he spent his final years in the town of Amboise. Despite his advanced age, he continued to work on various projects and experiments until he died in 1519.

What we know about Leonardo today is largely thanks to his extensive notebooks, which were filled with his observations, sketches, and ideas. These notebooks were not widely known until centuries after his death, when they were rediscovered and studied by scholars. They provide a fascinating glimpse into his mind and his endless curiosity.

Leonardo's influence can be seen in many aspects of our modern world, including art, science, architecture, and engineering. His legacy continues to inspire generations of artists and scientists to push the boundaries of knowledge and creativity.

Learning from Leonardo

Leonardo da Vinci was not only an incredible artist, scientist, and inventor but also a great teacher. Many artists and scholars learned from him and were inspired by his work. Today, we can learn valuable lessons from Leonardo's life and apply them to our own lives.

One of the most important lessons we can learn from Leonardo is the importance of curiosity. Leonardo was intensely curious about the world around him. He observed everything in great detail and asked questions about how things worked. He believed that curiosity was the key to unlocking knowledge and understanding. Leonardo also taught us the value of persistence and hard work. He spent countless hours studying and practicing his craft. He believed that mastery could only be achieved through continuous effort. Leonardo once said, "People of accomplishment rarely sat back and let things happen to them. They went out and happened to things."

Another lesson we can learn from Leonardo is the power of observation. He believed that the best way to understand something was to observe it carefully. Leonardo's meticulous observations of the human body and nature paved the way for advancements in both science and art.

Leonardo also emphasized the importance of learning from mistakes. He understood that failure is often a necessary part of the learning process. Leonardo once said, "I have offended God and mankind because my work didn't reach the quality it should have." However, he used his mistakes as opportunities for growth and improvement.

One of the most enduring lessons from Leonardo is the importance of interdisciplinary thinking. Leonardo believed that all knowledge was connected and that artists, scientists, and inventors should work together to gain a deeper understanding of the world. He combined art and science in a way that had never been done before.

Leonardo also taught us the value of imagination and thinking outside the box. He was not afraid to question established beliefs and explore new ideas. Leonardo encouraged others to embrace their creativity and let their imaginations soar.

Lastly, Leonardo's love for nature and the environment can teach us to appreciate and care for the world around us. He believed that nature held the answers to many of life's mysteries and that we should respect and protect it.

By learning from Leonardo's teachings, we can develop important skills such as curiosity, persistence, observation, learning from mistakes, interdisciplinary thinking, imagination, and environmental awareness. These skills can help us become better learners, thinkers, and creators.

So, let's take inspiration from Leonardo da Vinci and continue to explore, question, and discover the wonders of the world around us.

MARK LYLANI

CONCLUSION

As we come to the end of our journey through the incredible life of Leonardo Da Vinci, one thing becomes clear: Leonardo was much more than a master painter. He was a relentless explorer, a brilliant inventor, and a visionary who saw the world in ways that continue to inspire us centuries later.

From his humble beginnings in Vinci to his final years in France, Leonardo's life was a testament to the power of curiosity and the pursuit of knowledge. His artistic masterpieces like the "Mona Lisa" and "The Last Supper" have captivated audiences for generations. At the same time, his scientific and engineering sketches reveal a mind constantly pushing the boundaries of what was known and possible.

Leonardo's legacy is not just in the art he created or the inventions he dreamed up but in the way he approached life. He taught us the value of asking questions, of being curious about everything around us, and of never being afraid to combine art and science. His notebooks, filled with observations and ideas, remind us that learning is a lifelong journey.

As we reflect on Leonardo's achievements, let's remember that his greatness was rooted in his curiosity. Whether you're an aspiring artist, a budding scientist, or just a curious kid, Leonardo's life shows that with passion and perseverance, you can make amazing discoveries and create something truly extraordinary.

So, keep exploring, keep questioning, and let Leonardo Da Vinci's incredible story inspire you to follow your own curiosity. Who knows what amazing things you might achieve? The world is full of mysteries waiting to be uncovered, and just like Leonardo, you have the power to make your mark on history.

Made in the USA
Middletown, DE
01 December 2024